-UNOFFICIAL-

OVER 150 BLOCKBUSTER JOKES FOR CRAFTY KIDS OF ALL AGES!

by
Ava & Nico Gabriel
(With some help from Dad)

X-Blam Press
Los Angeles

Unofficial Jokecraft! Over 150 Blockbuster Jokes for Crafty Kids of All Ages! written by Ava and Nico Gabriel, Marcos Gabriel.

               p. cm.

  Summary: An unofficial collection of hilarious jokes based on the Minecraft universe. 1. Education – Juvenile jokes. 2. Young adult jokes, American. 3. Humorous, American. 4. Schools – Juvenile jokes. Gabriel, Ava and Nico. 2015

ISBN-13: 978-1514650967

ISBN-10: 1514650967

Printed in the United States of America.

For Minecraft fans who love to laugh their blocks off.

-UNOFFICIAL-

JOKECRAFT

OVER 150 BLOCKBUSTER JOKES FOR CRAFTY KIDS OF ALL AGES!

How do you know there's a chance three-headed monster will be in your area?

Check the *Wither Channel.*

What's a Minecraft player's favorite snack?

Notch-os.

Why did the Zombie Pigman cross the road?

Because he was riding a chicken.

Why do Cave Spiders live in caves?

Because apartments are too expensive!

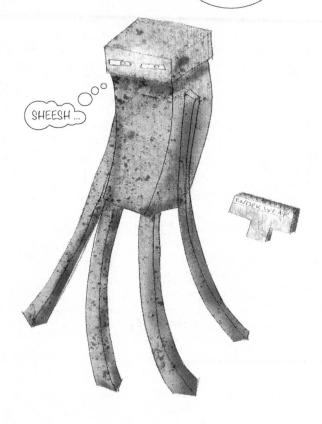

What's Steve's favorite kind of dance?

Square dancing.

How did the police catch the Redstone thief?

They caught him red-handed.

What'd Steve have in his shoe after a trip to the desert?

Sole sand.

Why was the Wither so smart?

Because three heads are better than one.

What's a Minecraft player's favorite cookie?

*Ore*os.

What's Herobrine's favorite kind of music?

Rock and *Troll*.

What do you call a Snow Golem in the desert?

A puddle.

What do you give your Wolf when it has a fever?

Ketchup! It's *great* on hot dogs!

What do Minecraft players want for Easter?

Marshmallow *Creeps*.

Why are Miners terrible at sharing?

Because everything they see is *Mine, Mine, Mine!*

What are Minecraft ducks afraid of?

The *Quack*-en.

Did you hear about the Creeper who became a huge rock star?

Yeah - he really *blew up.*

What sound does a Creeper Kitty make?

Creep-purrrrrrrrrrr.

Did you hear about the really evil Miner?

He was *rotten to the ore.*

Did you hear that Steve was having troubles hiding his treasure?

Yeah - he was having *chest pains.*

What do you call a Witch that spawns in the desert?

A *Sand-Witch!*

And what if that Witch is scared of everything?

A *Chicken* Sand-Witch!

What did the Zombie Pigman's wife say to her husband?

You take me for *grunted.*

What two drinks should you *never* have in Minecraft?

Tea and Tea.

Did you hear about the Creeper birthday party?

It was a real *blast!*

What do you call a Zombie Pigman that knows Karate?

A *Pork Chop!*

"I heard you wanted to have a small Minecraft party."
"Yeah, but you know how it goes - suddenly it was a whole block party!"

Did you hear about the player that spawned a ton of cats?

Yeah - he spawned oce*lots* and *lots* and *lots!*

Why is the Wither always asking questions?

'Cause he's not sure *wither* you will or *wither* you won't.

How did the Enderman get so strong?

He trained with all his Ender-might!

TONGUE TWISTERS!

Try saying these three times fast!

Billy built blocks bit by bit.

Skating Squids squawk silly songs.

Wooly wolves wash wobbly watermelons.

Steve smelt six silver swords.

Two Villagers were looking over a farm. The first Villager said, **"Wow - look at that bunch of cows."**

The second one said, "Herd."

"Heard of what?"

"Herd of cows."

"Well, of course I heard of cows! That's why I pointed out that bunch!"

Did you hear about the farmer who only planted blocks of hay?

He wanted *Straw*-berries!

Why didn't Steve get good grades?

Because he's a *blockhead.*

Where does a girl Creeper keep all her money?

In her *Cree-purse.*

How do you go to the bathroom in an Enderportal?

In a Portal-Potty.

Why can't you complain when you haven't spawned cows?

'Cause you got *no beef.*

Why did you trap a cow with all those ice blocks?

I wanted to make an *Eski-moo!*

Where do cows go on a date?

To the *moo*-vies.

What did the Wolf say when Steve stepped on his paw?

Ow-ow-ow-wooooooooooooooo!

Block, Block!

Who's there?

Sssssssssssss...

Sssssssssssss who?

BOOOOOOOOOOOOOM! (And make sure you do this *really loud!*)

MINECRAFT MOVIE TITLES (Part 1)

Ghastbusters

Enderdragon's Game

The Blaze Runner

Star Ores

Endermen in Black

The Nether-Ending Story

Where does the Enderdragon sit when he comes to dinner?

Anywhere he wants to!

Which creature is best at baseball?

Bats, of course.

How many tickles does it take to make a Squid laugh out loud?

*Ten*tacles.

What do you get when you spawn an angry sheep and an angry cow?

Two animals in a *baaaaaaad moooooooood.*

How do Spider Jockeys send emails?

Through their *World Wide Web!*

Did you hear about the Ocelot rock star?

Yeah! Her name's Kitty Purry!

What's the Kracken's favorite snack?

Fish and Ships.

Block, Block!

> Who's there?

Squid!

> Squid who?

Awww, Squid it ... you know who I am!

Did you hear about the Goldfish who lost most of his money?

> Now he's just a *Silver*fish.

Why did Steve put wood blocks on his bed?

> He wanted to sleep like a log!

Why did the player throw Slime?

Because *slime flies* when you're having fun!

"I invited my Minecraft plushies to lunch, but they didn't want to go."

"Why not?

"They were already *stuffed*."

Why is the Squid the best creature to take to war?

Because he's *well-armed*.

What do you call a Silverfish with no eyes?

A Slverfssssssh.

What do you call it when an Ocelot destroys your Village?

A cat-astrophe.

What kind of crackers does a Blaze like in its soup?

Firecrackers!

Block, Block!

Who's there?

Lettuce.

Lettuce who?

Lettuce in, there are Creepers out here!

Did you hear about the kid who could play Minecraft only using his brain?

He calls it *Mind-Craft*.

Where do Squid keep their money?

In the River Bank!

One Villager said to Steve, **"Man, I haven't slept for days."**

Steve said, "Why not?"

The Villager replied, **"Because I only sleep at night!"**

How do Snow Golems get to work?

By icicle.

What's the deadliest gem in the game?

Die-mond.

Why do you have to go to bed at night?

Because the bed won't go to you!

Why was the Wolf called Frost?

Because Frost *bites*!

What's the best way to catch a fish?

Have another player throw one at you.

What's as big as an Enderdragon but doesn't weigh anything?

The Enderdragon's shadow.

What do you get when you cross a snake with a Minecraft player?

A boa *constructor*.

How does a Villager count his cows?

With a *cow*-culator.

Block, Block!

Who's there?

Annie.

Annie who?

Annie body wanna play some Minecraft?

What's a Creeper's favorite class at school?

Hisssssssssss-tory.

What do you get when you cross wood blocks with Sheep?

Fur trees.

What instrument do Skeletons play?

Trom-*bone*.

Block, Block!

Who's there?

Wither!

Wither who?

I'm coming in, Wither you like it or not!

Why did the player place Wood Stairs near the Brick Stairs?

Because he wanted to have a stairing contest.

What kind of pet can you put in your buildings that won't eat, sleep, or make a mess?

Car-*pet.*

What do you get when an Enderdragon sneezes?

You get *out of the way!*

What does a Squid say when you spawn it in the desert?

"Long time no sea."

What can run around a whole village, but never move?

A fence.

What does a Miner wear to bed?

Gem-mies.

What's a Snow Golem's favorite dessert?

Ice-Scream.

Why did Steve win the argument with his Diamond Sword?

He had a good point.

What do you call a Skeleton that won't attack?

Lazy bones.

What do you call a Miner who tickles Enderdragons?

Crazy!

How do Squids make phone calls underwater?

With their *shell-phones*.

Why can't you trust a Squid?

Because there's always something fishy about them.

Did you hear about the new *Minecraft* movie?

They're calling it a real *Blockbuster!*

Block, Block!

Who's there?

Wood.

Wood who?

Wood you please open the door?

Why can't Silverfish play basketball?

They *always* stay away from the net.

What did Steve say to the impatient farmer?

"Just *wheat* a minute ..."

What do Spider Jockeys do at the Gym?

Spin class!

Why did the Ghast get a ticket?

It didn't have a haunting license.

Why didn't the Skeleton attack Steve?

It didn't have the guts.

What did the vine say to the wall?

"I got you covered."

TONGUE TWISTERS TWO!

Try saying these three times fast!

Crooked Crafters crumble quickly.

Big bad blocks block black boulders.

Pewee Pete picked a pack of puny pick-axes.

Silly Sally switched skins on Sunday.

What's a Witch's favorite subject in school?

Spelling.

Heard about the social network for Minecraft players?

It's called *Faceblock*.

Sister: **"I'm trying to play Minecraft, but my little brother is annoying me!"**
Dad: "He's not even playing with you!"
Sister: "I know! That's what's annoying me!"

You wanna drop by the Ghast's house?

Nah ... he's *nether* home.

Player: "I made my whole house out of cookie texture!"
Player 2: "How'd it turn out?"
Player: "A little *crummy.*"

What happened when the nervous player planted crops?

He got *edgy veggies.*

Why do Minecraft chickens watch the news?

To get the feather forecast.

Why did the slime cross the road?

It was stuck to the chicken's foot.

Why did the wolf scratch itself?

It had a *glitch.*

Why did the player put a mirror in front of his bed?

He wanted to see what he looked like when he was asleep.

Villager: **"I'm looking for a new furnace."**

Village Salesman: "How about this one?"

Villager: **"Is it popular?"**

Village Salesman: "Oh, yes! It's our best-*smelter!*"

What's the nicest way to greet a Wither?

Hello ... hello ... hello.

Did you hear about the cows that wrecked the village?

It was an *udder* catastrophe.

What did the sheep say when the player tried to shave it?

"Shear-iously?"

MINECRAFT MOVIE TITLES (Part 2)

Dude, Where's My Minecart?

How to Train Your Enderdragon

Polterghast

The Iron Golem

The Amazing SpiderJockey-Man

Lava, Actually

Did you hear about Steve's son?

They say he's a chip off the ol' block.

What's Steve's favorite kind of music?

Block and roll.

What do you get when you cross Gold Ore with a Chicken?

Chicken Nuggets.

Why's that Miner running away?

He got scared out of his *mine*.

How many items can you fit in an empty chest?

Only one … after that, it's no longer empty!

What does a Magma Cube take for a headache?

Ash-pirin.

Why is a Blaze a terrible boss?

He's always *firing* everyone.

Do you know which mob makes potions?

I dunno ... Witch?

How do Villagers fly across the land?

By *AirCraft.*

Why do Glowstones get A's in school?

Because they're very bright!

Why shouldn't you tell secrets in a Spider Cave?

Because the cave is bugged!

What goes *Ha! Ha! Ha! Plop!?*

A Zombie laughing its head off.

What's a Minecraft player's favorite color?

Ore-ange.

Hey! Who left this in the furnace?

You know what they say ...

whoever *smelt it, dealt it!*

Why can Zombie Pigmen write such beautiful music?

Because they're de-*composers*.

What do you call an Ocelot in the snow?

One cool cat.

How did Steve cut down the tree?

Axe-identally.

Why are Minecraft players terrible with decisions?

Because they could do this ... *ore* they could do that ... *ore* they could do something else!

What do you get when a cat attacks a pig?

An *Oce-lot* of bacon!

Why is it rude to invite a Wolf to dinner?

'Cause he's only gonna *wolf* it down!

How do Zombie Pigmen pass secret messages?

With invisible *oink*.

SIGNS YOU *MIGHT* PLAY TOO MUCH MINECRAFT

[ ] You punch trees *in real life.*

[ ] You won't turn off the lights when you go to sleep because you *know* a Creeper might spawn there.

[ ] You insist on always carrying 64 items in your backpack.

[ ] You're afraid to dig too deep in your backyard because you *know* you'll hit lava.

SIGNS YOU *MIGHT* PLAY TOO MUCH MINECRAFT

[ ] You know your friends by their usernames, not their *real names.*

[ ] You say names like "Stampy" and "Ballistic Squid" like it's totally normal.

[ ] You hear songs on the radio and are like "Hey! I know this song!" But then realize you only know the *Minecraft* version.

SIGNS YOU *MIGHT* PLAY TOO MUCH MINECRAFT

[ ] When your dad gets ready to grill, you beg him for the coal.

[ ] When the sun sets, you *immediately* get into your bed.

[ ] Your parents have caught you trying to dig a tunnel *under the house*.

[ ] You've spent an entire day in your pajamas. Building stuff. In Minecraft.

SIGNS YOU *MIGHT* PLAY TOO MUCH MINECRAFT

[ ] You can't understand why it takes so long for trees to grow in the real world.

[ ] You're pretty sure you could fill a swimming pool with just a couple buckets of water.

[ ] Update day is like the *greatest day ever*.

[ ] You've punched a sheep at a petting zoo, hoping for wool.

SIGNS YOU *MIGHT* PLAY TOO MUCH MINECRAFT

[ ] *Jokecraft* is totally your favorite book!

65032057R00051

Made in the USA
San Bernardino, CA
26 December 2017